C000149013

Edinburgh

Compiled by
Terry Marsh

JARROLD
publishing

Mapping
sourced from

Ordnance
Survey

Text: Terry Marsh
Photography: Terry Marsh
Editor: James Hopkin
Designer: Douglas Whitworth
© Jarrold Publishing 2003

OS Ordnance Survey This product includes mapping data licensed from Ordnance Survey® with the permission of the Controller of Her Majesty's Stationery Office. © Crown Copyright 2002. All rights reserved. Licence number 100017593. Ordnance Survey, the OS symbol and Pathfinder are registered trademarks and Explorer, Landranger and Outdoor Leisure are trademarks of the Ordnance Survey, the national mapping agency of Great Britain.

Jarrold Publishing ISBN 0-7117-2427-X

While every care has been taken to ensure the accuracy of the route directions, the publishers cannot accept responsibility for errors or omissions, or for changes in details given. The countryside is not static: hedges and fences can be removed, field boundaries can alter, footpaths can be rerouted and changes in ownership can result in the closure or diversion of some concessionary paths. Also, paths that are easy and pleasant for walking in fine conditions may become slippery, muddy and difficult in wet weather, while stepping-stones across rivers and streams may become impassable.

If you find an inaccuracy in either the text or maps, please write or e-mail Jarrold Publishing at one of the addresses below.

First published 2003
by Jarrold Publishing

Printed in Belgium
by Proost NV, Turnhout. 1/03

Jarrold Publishing
Pathfinder Guides, Whitefriars,
Norwich NR3 1TR

E-mail: pathfinder@jarrold.com
www.jarrold-publishing.co.uk

Front cover: Carnethy Hill
Previous page: Wildlife Garden, Glencorse

Contents

Keymap

SCALE 1:312 500 or 1 INCH to 5 MILES *1CM to 3.1 KM*

| 0 | 2 | 4 | 6 | 8 | 10 KILOMETRES | 15 |

| 0 | 2 | 4 | 6 MILES 8 | 10 |

KEYMAP HEIGHTS SHOWN IN FEET

Introduction

The routes and information in this book have been devised specifically with families and children in mind. All the walks include points of interest as well as a question to provide an objective.

If you, or your children, have not walked before, choose from the shorter walks for your first outings, though only a few of the walks are especially demanding. The purpose is not simply to get from A to B, but to enjoy an exploration, which may be just a steady stroll in the countryside, alongside rivers and lakes, through woodlands or climbing hills.

The walks are graded by length and difficulty, but few landscapes are truly flat, so even short walks may involve some ascent, though this is nowhere excessive, and even the height gain among the Pentland Hills walks will succumb to a steady plod. Details are given under Route Features in the first information box for each route. But the precise nature of the ground underfoot will depend on recent weather conditions.

West Kip

If you do set out on a walk and discover the going is harder than you expected, or the weather has deteriorated, do not be afraid to turn back. The route will always be there another day, when you are fitter or the children are more experienced or the weather is better. Few of the walks in this book involve rough terrain (though there are a number of steep grassy slopes, a few exposed summits and some muddy going after rain), but it is always advisable to wear proper walking footwear rather than trainers or wellington boots, and to take wind- or water-proofs.

Bear in mind that the countryside is constantly changing. Landmarks may disappear, gates may becomes stiles, rights-of-way, such as they are in Scotland, may be altered, permissive paths may close. In quite a few places the terrain can be confusing, and this means having to pay rather close attention to route descriptions and waymarking or, in the absence of waymarking, the general direction followed by the path. But none of the walks is so complex as to deter anyone.

A few of the paths are seasonally overgrown, or may be affected with wind-damage. This presents two problems: one is difficulty in following the route underfoot; the other is the soaking you may get from overgrowth if you do the walk after rain, or stinging by nettles, which will be a problem for young children and also makes the wearing of shorts something to be wary of.

Because many of the walks venture into remote areas of woodland, moorland or mountainside it is a good idea to get into the habit of carrying a small daysack containing waterproof clothing, spare clothing against a chill wind, something to eat and drink (preferably a warm drink, though bottled water is fine on a hot summer's day). And always take a map and compass, and the knowledge to use them safely; if you are not expert with maps, these walks generally would be a good place to develop your skills.

Around Edinburgh
The walks featured in this book are all south of the Firth of Forth and range from the most westerly around Linlithgow and Beecraigs Country Park to the most easterly at North Berwick. In a southerly direction, they

embrace the Pentland Hills, reaching down as far as Carlops and the North Esk Reservoir.

It has been a pleasure to compile this selection of walks, but especially to talk to the many helpful people along the way who have enthused about 'their patch', be it Almondell and Calderwood Country Park, Dalkeith Country Park, Rosslyn Chapel or the Red Moss Nature Reserve. As they say, 'it's good to talk', and talking to the people I encountered in these places and out on the hills has only served to tell me what a wonderful and diverse repertoire Edinburgh and its environs holds for those who enjoy walking in Britain's countryside.

The most amazing place of all was undoubtedly Rosslyn Chapel. Here, an intended 'longer' walk became so entangled in the beauty of the chapel, the history of the nearby inn, graveyard and castle, that plans were changed to allow time to take it all in. The same, in a sense, was true of Aberlady Bay. Here, bad weather forced a reconsideration, and that was when Aberlady Bay Nature Reserve played its ace, and lured me into a fabulous region of wild flowers, birds, insects and the occasional stoat. Anyone with an interest in natural history should visit Aberlady at some stage, especially during the flowering months.

Carving at entrance of Bavelaw Reserve

Not far from Aberlady, Gullane Bay was a complete contrast: not that it didn't have the same appeal or the same diversity, but here the focus was out into the Firth of Forth, watching seabirds and hoping for the odd inquisitive porpoise or dolphin.

In the west, Linlithgow church is a gem, its carvings and

In the wooded confines of Corstorphine Hill

stained glass windows sure to inspire all but the most hard-hearted – you don't have to be a churchgoer to appreciate the skill and patience of the craftsmen who built this magnificent building. And in a totally different sense, the same is true of Beecraigs Country Park and the lovely little hill of Cockleroy. It was an intentional decision to devise the walk so that the splendid adventure play area at Bal Vormie wasn't encountered until near the end of the walk, otherwise mums and dads would simply be sitting around all day.

It was, of course, impossible to write a book of walks based on Edinburgh and to ignore the Pentland Hills. This stunning range of domed, grassy summits offers so much potential, so much opportunity for exercise and open-air enjoyment, and such a sense of invigorating freedom that at one stage it looked as though all the walks would be in the Pentlands. But sense prevailed. Even so, the opportunity to learn the fundamental skills of hillwalking among the Pentlands before venturing into the rather higher summits that Scotland has to offer, has not been ignored. Nor has Edinburgh's own 'summit' been omitted. Arthur's Seat must be the most-ascended hill in Britain, and not without good cause for it exemplifies everything that is good about walking around Edinburgh.

1 *Roslin Glen*

START Roslin
DISTANCE 1 mile (1.6km)
TIME 1 hour
PARKING Roslin Glen Country Park
ROUTE FEATURES Woodland paths, lanes, steep steps

There is far more to explore in the heavily wooded Roslin Glen than is visited on this walk, but this brief introduction is so full of interest that it consumes far more than the allocated time.

Leave the car park and turn right along the road, soon crossing the River North Esk, and then immediately turning right onto a signposted path that leads to a wooded flight of steps known as Jacob's Ladder.

At the top of the steps Ⓐ, turn right alongside a road for a few strides then re-enter the woodland of Roslin Glen at its upper boundary. The woodland here is mainly oak and hosts a wide range of wild flowers from the heady scented wild garlic to red campion, germander speedwell, bluebells, dog's mercury and celandine.

The woodland path emerges close by a graveyard. Walk up a lane to a T-junction, and there turn right at what used to be the Rosslyn Inn.

Rosslyn Chapel was founded in 1446 by Sir William St Clair, the third and last St Clair Prince of Orkney; it has remained in the same family since its foundation, though the church was never fully completed. This is Scotland's most outstanding Gothic church, and is famed for its ornate carvings, both internal and external, and its lovely stained glass windows.

PUBLIC TRANSPORT Buses to Roslin
REFRESHMENTS Tea shop at Rosslyn Chapel
PUBLIC TOILETS None on route, but toilets in Rosslyn Chapel shop for visitors
ORDNANCE SURVEY MAPS Explorer 344 (Pentland Hills, Penicuik & West Lothian), Landranger 66 (Edinburgh & Midlothian area)

Continue a little further to the shop entrance to Rosslyn Chapel **B** (admission charge).

Go back to the T-junction and turn left down to the graveyard and there turn left again onto a stony track between the graveyard sections, passing an ancient well on

The Apprentice Pillar, interior Rosslyn Chapel

Rosslyn Castle

the left before reaching the gates of Rosslyn Castle **C**, now used as self-catering holidays lets. Go through the gates to get a better view of the castle.

> **?** *Can you discover which famous people visited Rosslyn Inn.*

Just before the castle gates, turn right down a steep flight of steps that leads back into woodland.

At the bottom of the steps, go forward to and across a footbridge spanning the river. Over the bridge bear immediately right and shortly right again to return to the car park.

●

North Berwick Law

START North Berwick
DISTANCE 1½ miles (2km)
HEIGHT GAIN 482 ft (147m)
TIME 1 hour
PARKING Car park at start
ROUTE FEATURES Tracks and very steep paths, exposed summit

North Berwick Law, the core of an ancient volcano, is a stunning viewpoint, the most prominent landmark in East Lothian, and more than justifies the effort in clambering to its summit.

Begin by passing through a narrow gap to the right of a gate and turn along a broad track.

Shortly, a steep grassy path appears on the left rising onto the Law Ⓐ. This is the way to go, it is very steep, but the ascent does ease after a while.

North Berwick Law provides a fine panoramic view of the Fife coastline, the Firth of Forth and the Lothians. There is evidence of human occupation on the hill since the Iron Age, possibly extending into the Middle Ages.

Rosebay Willowherd: North Berwick Law provides an ideal habitat for wild flowers

PUBLIC TRANSPORT Buses and trains to North Berwick
REFRESHMENTS North Berwick
PICNIC AREA At start
PUBLIC TOILETS None on route
ORDNANCE SURVEY MAPS Explorer 351 (Dunbar & North Berwick), Landranger 66 (Edinburgh & Midlothian area)

The way to the top is not in doubt, the path zigzagging a little to take the sting out of the climb.

From the summit, the safest way down is to retrace the outward route.

Cotton thistle: the national emblem of Scotland

? *There used to be a look-out point on the top of North Berwick Law. What was it constructed to 'look out' for?*

Arthur's Seat

START Meadowbank
DISTANCE 2 miles (3.2km)
TIME 1 hour
PARKING Meadowbank (Free)
ROUTE FEATURES Park road, steep climb and descent, rocky paths

3

Arthur's Seat is quite possibly the most-ascended hill in Britain. Its location, near the heart of the city, makes it a natural target for walkers, joggers, cyclists of all shapes and sizes, and it is unlikely that you will ever find yourself entirely alone here.

🖉 Begin from the car park at Meadowbank, not far from St Margaret's Loch and go up steps at the far side to reach the surfaced (one-way) Queen's Drive.

Follow this as it climbs steadily and diverts around Dunsapie Hill, site of an Iron Age fort, to reach Dunsapie Loch Ⓐ, which is always popular with swans and wildfowl. Walk past the loch to reach a car park.

From the car park beyond the end of Dunsapie Loch, cross the road (Queen's Drive) with care, and

Arthur's Seat

PUBLIC TRANSPORT Buses to Meadowbank
REFRESHMENTS Meadowbank
PUBLIC TOILETS None on route
ORDNANCE SURVEY MAPS Explorer 350 (Edinburgh, Musselburgh & Queensferry), Landranger 66 (Edinburgh & Midlothian area)

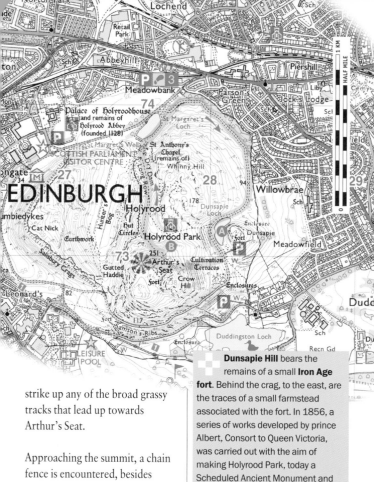

strike up any of the broad grassy tracks that lead up towards Arthur's Seat.

Approaching the summit, a chain fence is encountered, besides which a rocky path leads up to the trig pillar on the summit and the nearby topograph which identifies the features of the surrounding countryside.

From the summit, go back down to the lower end of the chain fence, and there, bear left onto a path **B**

Dunsapie Hill bears the remains of a small **Iron Age fort**. Behind the crag, to the east, are the traces of a small farmstead associated with the fort. In 1856, a series of works developed by prince Albert, Consort to Queen Victoria, was carried out with the aim of making Holyrood Park, today a Scheduled Ancient Monument and Site of Special Scientific Interest, more pleasant for recreation. The lochs at Dunsapie and Meadowbank were created when the road was built.

descending into a narrow valley. The path is initially steep, and steep again towards the end of the

The view from the top of **Arthur's Seat** is outstanding, embracing the Kingdom of Fife across the Firth of Forth, out to Bass Rock and round to the Pentland Hills: virtually the whole of the city of Edinburgh is mapped out at your feet. This is a spectacular and rewarding place to be at any time of year. The summit is occupied by the site of another Iron Age hillfort, larger than that on Dunsapie Hill.

valley, but between the two sections drops gently through a peaceful mini-glen that could be a million miles from the busy city nearby.

At the foot of the valley, bear right to St Margaret's Loch, beneath the ruins of St Anthony's Chapel, thought to date from the 16th century and to have been founded by the Hospitallers of St Anthony.

Walk to the right of St Margaret's Loch, and on the far side take the right-hand one of two paths, walking out to the start of Queen's Drive. Go across this to return to the car park. ●

By what name was Queen's Drive formerly known?

The summit of Arthur's Seat

4 Almondell and Calderwood Country Park

START East Calder
DISTANCE 2¼ miles (3.6km)
TIME 1–1¼ hours
PARKING Car park at East Calder entrance
ROUTE FEATURES Woodland trails, riverside paths

Concealed in the valley of the River Almond, this lovely country park is full of interest and has a fascinating history. It is based on two adjoining estates – Almondell and Calderwood – and can be a very time-consuming place to explore in spite of its modest size, but eminently enjoyable.

Begin from the car park on the edge of East Calder by walking back towards the entrance, but soon turning right onto a woodland footpath that emerges at an information panel adjoining a surfaced estate road. Turn right and follow the road, flanked by hazel, ash, hawthorn, elder, wild cherry, copper beech and sycamore, as far as the crenellated Almondell Bridge Ⓐ.

Recently restored, **Almondell Bridge** is otherwise known as Nasmyth Bridge after its designer **Alexander Nasmyth**, the landscape painter believed to be the only painter to have accomplished an authenticated portrait of **Robert Burns**.

Immediately before the bridge, turn right onto an ascending woodland path that leads through delightful mixed woodland to meet a higher path along the top edge. Turn left along this.

The path runs on along the top edge of the woodland, and then turns back into the body of the woodland, going down a long flight of steps to emerge at a path

PUBLIC TRANSPORT Buses to East Calder
REFRESHMENTS Visitor Centre
PUBLIC TOILETS In walled garden
ORDNANCE SURVEY MAPS Explorer 350 (Edinburgh, Musselburgh & Queensferry), Landranger 65 (Falkirk & West Lothian)

not far from a suspension bridge built in 1970 by the Royal Engineers **B**.

From the bridge go forward alongside the walled garden (toilets) and ascend gently to a surfaced road (red waymark). Turn left and walk to the visitor centre housed in what was the coach house and stables.

Heading into Almondell Country Park

Almondell Bridge

Continue past the visitor centre, following the surfaced road until it returns to Almondell Bridge. Once again, do not cross the bridge, but go to the right of it on a descending track that runs along the wooded banks of the River Almond.

When the red waymarked route bears left, turn with it, walking across a footbridge with an aqueduct suspended beneath it **C**.

On the other side of the river, turn right, climbing steps onto a path high above the river. When the path forks, branch left, and shortly left again through woodland to rejoin the main surfaced driveway. Turn right and walk back to the information panel, and there keep left through woodland to return to the car park. ●

> **?** *Can you find anything that might help you see stars?*

> Built in 1820 at the time of the construction of the Union Canal, the **aqueduct** takes the form of a trough on a cantilevered support slung beneath the footbridge. It carries the canal feeder stream over the **River Almond**.

Holyrood Park

START Duddingston
DISTANCE 2¼ miles (3.6km)
TIME 1 hour
PARKING Car park at Duddingston Loch
ROUTE FEATURES Roads, stony tracks, ascent and descent, field paths

5

This is an easy and delightful wander around part of Holyrood Park, and overlooks the Palace of Holyrood House, the official residence of the Queen when she is in Edinburgh. The walk does not visit the Palace, but it is only a short detour off-route should anyone wish to include it.

Begin from the car park near the Duddingston entrance to the park and turn right along the roadside footpath above Duddingston Loch.

Continue along the road until an open grassed area appears on the right, along with the summit of Arthur's Seat. Here, cross the road with care and walk over the grassed area, bearing slightly right to cross another road (Queen's Drive) and a stony track bearing right towards a gap Ⓐ between the mound of Arthur's Seat and a long line of crags (Salisbury Crags) on the left.

Duddingston Loch is a nature reserve, and the favoured haunt of a good population of wildfowl, especially in winter when greylag and Canada geese gather here. Above the road, on the right, steep crags rise. These are known as **Samson's Ribs**, and are mainly basalt rock, similar to that found on the islands of Ulva and Staffa off Mull.

Turn left along a stony track that climbs steadily along the base of Salisbury Crags, giving a splendid, airy view over the city of Edinburgh to the Pentland Hills.

Soon the path levels and then begins to descend steeply, finally

PUBLIC TRANSPORT Buses to park entrance at St Leonard's
REFRESHMENTS St Leonard's
PUBLIC TOILETS None on route
ORDNANCE SURVEY MAPS Explorer 350 (Edinburgh, Musselburgh & Queensferry), Landranger 66 (Edinburgh & Midlothian area)

Salisbury Crags were once quarried to provide stone for the streets of London, and the path that runs below them is known as the Radical Road, so-called because of a proposal by **Sir Walter Scott**, who expressed concern at the burgeoning radicalism of the unemployed in the city following the Napoleonic Wars. He hoped that putting men to work constructing this pathway would divert their minds from dissent.

reaching a road **B** near the grounds of Holyrood House. Here, do not cross the road, but bear right on the upper of two surfaced pathways.

Gradually the path turns into a valley known as Hunter's Bog, with Arthur's Seat rising formidably on the left. When the

The Palace of Holyrood House

surfacing ends, keep forward, climbing gently.

The path, flanked by a wealth of wild flowers in spring passes a lochan and rises steadily to a gap between Arthur's Seat and the end

Duddingston Loch

of Salisbury Crags, which from this side present only a grassy posterior.

Go through the gap and bear left to rejoin Queen's Drive, and follow this for a little over half-a-mile (1km). When a fence, on the right, comes to an end, near a bench, go down a field path on the right, initially stepped, that leads to a wall. Turn right beside the wall and go down steps to emerge at a road near the Duddingston entrance to the park and only a few strides from the car park. ●

 Of what do you need to beware on this walk?

6 *Corstorphine Hill*

START Corstorphine
DISTANCE 2¼ miles (3.7km)
TIME 1–1½ hours
PARKING End of Cairnmuir Road
ROUTE FEATURES Woodland paths

Corstorphine Hill is a lovely place to wander, but not a place to practise navigation. The complexity of paths on this elongated wooded ridge overlooking Edinburgh is such that meaningful route description is difficult to come by. But that, in a way, is part of the attraction, as are the views across the city.

Begin from the parking area at the end of Cairnmuir Road and walk into the woodland, a local nature reserve. Take the first opportunity to branch left, climbing into an open area. Here the path forks; take that going forward into scrub, and then bear left gradually climbing towards the top of a radio mast that can be seen above the trees. Close by stands the Corstorphine Hill Tower **Ⓐ**.

Corstorphine Hill Tower was erected in 1871 by William Macfie to mark the centenary of Sir Walter Scott's birth. It was presented to the city in 1932 on the centenary of his death. The tower is occasionally open, on summer Sundays.

From the tower, the route finding has great potential for confusion. A broad track sets off from the tower, descending and then re-ascending. But after that numerous paths come and go so much so that it becomes impossible to be precise about directions. This doesn't matter: the best approach is to stay as high as possible, heading northwards along the ridge, and always taking the most prominent pathway.

PUBLIC TRANSPORT Buses to Corstorphine
REFRESHMENTS Corstorphine
PUBLIC TOILETS None on route
ORDNANCE SURVEY MAPS Explorer 350 (Edinburgh, Musselburgh and Queensferry), Landranger 66 (Edinburgh & Midlothian area)

Eventually, and there will be an eventually, the various paths all intercept a clear and prominent path **B**, obviously constructed rather than devised by the passage of feet. Where this is encountered, turn right along it; it provides a lovely route back along the eastern

Fungi love the shady, damp conditions of Corstorphine Hill

View over Edinburgh from Corstorphine Hill

flank of Corstorphine Hill, and brooks no argument about where it is going.

Finally, this reassuring path divides below a steep slope **C**, with a post and wire fence below it on the left. Here, bear right, and soon go back up in the general direction of the tower. But when the track goes left again, follow it, for a short while running along the boundary of the zoo, but then rejoining the outward route a short distance from the start.

●

> **?** *Woodland like this is a haven for squirrels. See if you can spot any.*

Linlithgow Loch

START Linlithgow
DISTANCE 2½ miles (4km)
TIME 1 hour
PARKING Linlithgow
ROUTE FEATURES Lochside and field paths

7

This tour of Linlithgow Loch is simple and straightforward, allowing ample opportunity to study the wild flowers that flank the water's edge and the wildfowl that find the loch to be a perfect habitat. The ruins of Linlithgow Palace and the beauty of St Michael's Church are an added bonus.

Begin from Linlithgow Cross and walk up Kirkgate towards the palace and through the gateway. Immediately turn left onto a surfaced path descending to the lochside. When the path meets

Linlithgow Palace was a popular place of residence with the Stuart kings and the birthplace of **Mary, Queen of Scots**. Work on the palace was started by James I of Scotland in 1425. The adjacent Church of St Michael, which largely dates from the 15th and 16th centuries, ranks among the finest buildings in Scotland.

another, go left and pass through a gate at the water's edge.

Continue now simply following the lochside path, which passes an area heavily populated by swans a-preening and greylag geese. The loch itself supports a good population of breeding coot, tufted duck and mallard, along with a few less common visitors.

Gradually the lochside path leads round to a footbridge **A** after which bear right, passing houses. When the surfaced pathway ends

PUBLIC TRANSPORT Buses and rail to Linlithgow
REFRESHMENTS Linlithgow
PUBLIC TOILETS Linlithgow
PLAY AREA Linlithgow Park
ORDNANCE SURVEY MAPS Explorer 349 (Falkirk, Cumbernauld & Livingston), Landranger 65 (Falkirk & West Lothian)

Stained glass window, Linlithgow Church

keep forward, still parallel with the water's edge. The path along the northern shore of the loch is a good place to look for wild flowers, among them cotton thistle (the heraldic emblem of Scotland), hardheads, blue comfrey, meadow cranesbill, ragwort, speedwell, chickweed, wild strawberries and white dead nettle.

When the path emerges at a road **B**, turn immediately right through a wooden gate and cross a

View across Linlithgow Loch

lochside meadow pastured by sheep. The ongoing path meets the main road. Here, turn right until, just before St Michael's Catholic Church, an enclosed path takes the route back into Linlithgow Park. Bear left, passing a children's play area, and walk across towards the palace.

St Michael's Church is a magnificent building and worth exploring. Its stained glass windows are delightful and there are a number of 'Consecration Crosses' carved into its walls, marking the places where the consecration water of Bishop de Bernham is said to have fallen at the time of the dedication of the original building in 1242.

Return through the gateway and back down Kirkgate to the start. ●

> **?** *One of the less well-known visitors to Linlithgow Loch is the ruddy duck. Can you spot any?*

8 *Vogrie Country Park*

Within a comparatively small area this charming country park, fashioned from the remains of the Vogrie Estate, boasts a wide range of attractions from simple woodland walks to the turmoil of a huge adventure play area, or a miniature railway.

START Vogrie
DISTANCE 2½ miles (4km)
TIME 2 hours
PARKING Car park at Hardwick (Charge between 1030 and 1930)
ROUTE FEATURES Woodland trails

Unusual seat Vogrie Country Park

Leave the car park by walking along a broad track to the left of the play area, but almost immediately leave it by turning onto a woodland path that runs through a long strip of broad-leaved woodland between the road and meadows.

Vogrie Country Park consists largely of the grounds of Vogrie House that were laid out in the 18th and 19th centuries. The park today is little changed from its original state, but forms only a small part of that estate. The original house was demolished and a new one built on the site in 1877.

PUBLIC TRANSPORT Buses along B6372
REFRESHMENTS Tea shop in country park
PLAY AREA Play area at start, and adventure play area near Vogrie House
PUBLIC TOILETS At start and near adventure play area
ORDNANCE SURVEY MAPS Explorer 345 (Lammermuir Hills, Dalkeith, Bonnyrigg & Gifford), Landranger 66 (Edinburgh & Midlothian area)

The path later descends to run alongside the road, and then swings back across the wooded shelter belt to run beside a meadow.

The path moves away gently from the road to a path junction 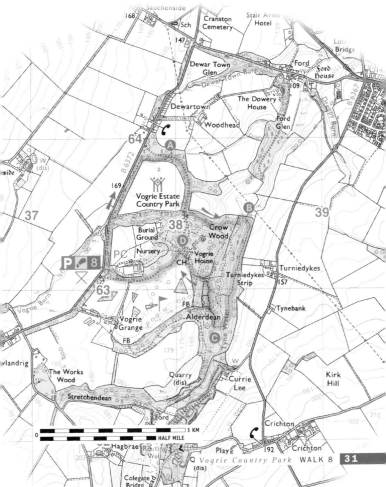Ⓐ. Here turn right (signposted for Vogrie House).

At a track junction, turn left following the course of a burn. Cross a footbridge and continue following the burn, later re-crossing the burn and turning right to cross the River Tyne Ⓑ.

Follow the ongoing path as it climbs easily to the top of a ridge

Vogrie House

and the edge of the woodland. On leaving the woodland go across grassland; ignore the first diverging path on the right, but take the next one which goes down to a bridge spanning the Tyne **C**.

Beyond, a zigzag path leads up into Alderdean Woods, cross another burn and then keep forward for Vogrie House.

From the front of Vogrie House cross to a small pond opposite **D**, which is an interesting place to spend some time with children.

Then walk along the main driveway, heading away from Vogrie House, eventually returning to the walled garden (now a garden centre) and the car park. ●

> **?** *Can you find any giant chairs?*

Castlelaw and Glencorse

START Flotterstone
DISTANCE 3¼ miles (5.3km)
TIME 2 hours
PARKING Flotterstone
ROUTE FEATURES Hill farm, hillfort site, upland tracks, lanes, woodland

9

This popular walk through Robert Louis Stevenson country to the Glencorse Reservoir takes the opportunity to visit an Iron Age hillfort on the flanks of Flotterstone Glen, and returns beside the reservoir before making a visit to a wildlife garden.

Beside the path near the start a plaque, placed by the Institute of Physics and the Royal Meteorological Society, commemorates **C T R Wilson**, born at Crosshouse Farm, Glencorse in 1869, the inventor of the **cloud chamber**.

Leave the car park by walking past the visitor centre and following a constructed pathway through a linear roadside woodland strip.

When the path emerges onto a road, keep right, following the road to a point, just beyond the end of a stand of Scots pine on the right, where a signposted shale path (for Castlelaw) heads up through gorse above a shallow ravine Ⓐ.

At the top of the path, at a T-junction, turn right (signposted for Castlelaw) along a broad track around the edge of a military training area, and leading to Castlelaw Farm.

At the entrance to the farm, turn right through a gate to follow a

PUBLIC TRANSPORT Buses to Flotterstone Bridge
REFRESHMENTS Pub at Flotterstone
PICNIC AREA Near start (small)
PUBLIC TOILETS At start and at Castlelaw car park
ORDNANCE SURVEY MAPS Explorer 344 (Pentland Hills, Penicuik & West Linton), Landranger 66 (Edinburgh & Midlothian area)

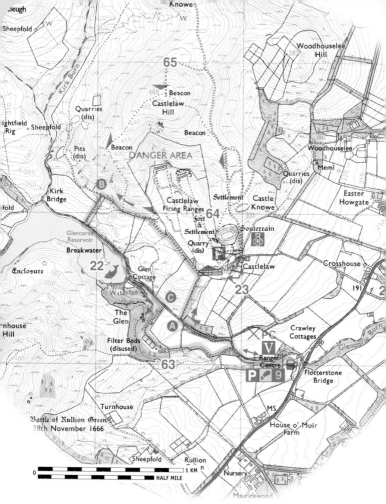

path around the farm, emerging at the end of a surfaced lane, near the Castlelaw car park.

Pass through a gate and walk up a stony track, as far as the fenced site of the hillfort, turning in through a gap.

From the hillfort return to its car park and walk back around the farm and out along the track to the T-junction at which this extension to Castlelaw began. Now keep forward along the broad track (signposted for Glencorse Reservoir).

A road track now takes the route on towards the reservoir, passing along the perimeter of the training area (marked by red and white banded poles).

Continue with the track, which eventually moves away from the training area and climbs easily for a short while to reach a signpost at the edge of a small plantation **B**. Here, leave the track by turning through a gate and walking down and within the edge of the plantation.

At the bottom, emerge onto the reservoir service road and turn left, following this out past Glen Cottage.

The **Iron Age fort** at **Castlelaw** is an excellent example of the kind of domestic settlement that was populated in the 1st millennium BC. Excavation at Castle Law has revealed a long history of fortification, and there would have been a sizeable farming community here.

The adjacent **Earth House** was not a dwelling but a cellar built partially underground; such structures are widespread throughout Scotland, and represent a tradition that began in the Northern isles about 400 years before Christ. The Earth House here was in use in the 2nd century AD, by which time the role of the hillfort was domestic rather than defensive.

Near the end of a wall **C**, leave the road (now surfaced) by turning

Glencorse Reservoir

Wild flowers near Glencorse Reservoir

into the edge of woodland on a descending path signposted to Flotterstone via the Old Filter Beds.

After an initial descent the path runs alongside Glencorse Burn, having earlier provided a lovely retrospective view of a waterfall.

See if you can discover what you should plant.

The path shortly bears away from the burn and passes a wildlife garden which is constructed on the site of one of the old filter beds.

A grassy path leads past the filter beds to two kissing-gates, and continues beyond between fences to meet a road. There turn right, but a few strides later bear left onto the woodland path used at the start of the walk, which leads back to the visitor centre. ●

Gullane Bay

START Gullane
DISTANCE 3½ miles
(5.7km)
TIME 2 hours
PARKING Gullane Bents
(Charge)
ROUTE FEATURES
Foreshore, sand dunes,
coastal links, trails

Gullane Bay is an inviting and shapely crescent of sandy beach backed by vegetated dunes. This is a popular place with migrant birds, but the flowers here are just as profuse, making Gullane another perfect place to study the natural history (see also Walk 12).

Walk through the car park and past a barrier, going down a track to the toilets and picnic area. Follow the descending track onto the foreshore and turn right.

The dunes of **Gullane Bay** are colonised by scentless mayweed, ragwort, viper's bugloss, sea aster and woody nightshade. This is a good place to look seaward, too, where eiders in various stages of moult gather in small groups around the rocks and further out. Once the winter months approach, this is an ideal spot to find sheltering shore birds like sanderling, sandpiper, oystercatcher and curlew.

Viper's bugloss, Gullane Bay

PUBLIC TRANSPORT Buses to Gullane
REFRESHMENTS Gullane
PUBLIC TOILETS Near start
ORDNANCE SURVEY MAPS Explorer 351 (Dunbar & North Berwick),
Landranger 66 (Edinburgh & Midlothian area)

Walk the entire length of Gullane Bay, and on the far side, at Black Rocks **A**, stay on a narrow path between the rocks and the base of the dunes.

As the northern tip of a plantation on the right is reached, so the path moves away from the shore to a ruined building **B** and turns

inland initially alongside a dilapidated wall. Follow a series of linked paths that run roughly parallel with the plantation boundary.

Gradually the path works a way round to the edge of Muirfield Golf Course, one of Scotland's great championship courses.

? *See how many different types of shell you can find on the beach.*

At the edge of the course the ongoing path becomes a vehicle track skirting the golf course. Continue to a placard that begins a narrow path **C** to the village of Gullane. Cutting through scrub and seasonally overgrown, this follows a perimeter fence and provides ample opportunity to study the flowers and shrubs.

Eventually the path merges with a broader, sandy bridleway **D**. Turn left.

The bridleway finally emerges onto a broad track at the north-eastern end of Gullane Bents. Turn right along this and follow it back to the starting point of the walk at the car park. ●

Gullane Bay

11 *Beecraigs Country Park*

START Beecraigs
DISTANCE 3¾ miles (6km)
TIME 2 hours
PARKING At visitor centre
ROUTE FEATURES
Woodland trails, lochside
paths, hill summit
(modest ascent)

The area of Beecraigs Country Park is put to full and good use, providing a wide range of activities from cycling and angling to archery and pony-trekking. This walk takes the opportunity to visit the adjacent summit viewpoint of Cockleroy. The route is waymarked throughout, which is a help as the woodland paths can be confusing.

From the car park set off along the signposted 'Deer Walkway', which leads through

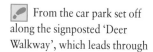
Beecraigs Loch is a long-established picturesque loch where brown trout fishing first took place in 1922. In recent times, the best brown trout caught was a fish of 8lbs 5oz, but these days the loch is stocked with rainbow trout from the nearby farm. The paths in the country park are flanked by a good range of wild flowers including selfheal, meadow cranesbill, speedwell, ox-eye daisy, rosebay and broad-leaved willowherb.

large pens containing herds of red deer, and follow the track down to enter the woodland of Beecraigs.

In the woodland, bear left alongside the loch, passing an information panel about a badger sett. The route is here waymarked with red arrows: if in doubt, follow these.

The path leads onto the dam of the loch, but then leaves it to go down steps to the entrance to Beecraigs Trout Farm. Walk away from the

PUBLIC TRANSPORT Buses and rail to Linlithgow
REFRESHMENTS Restaurant at nearby caravan site; seasonal snack bar at Bal Vormie play area
PUBLIC TOILETS At start and near Bal Vormie mill pond
PLAY AREA At Bal Vormie
ORDNANCE SURVEY MAPS Explorer 349 (Falkirk, Cumbernauld & Livingston), Landranger 65 (Falkirk & West Lothian)

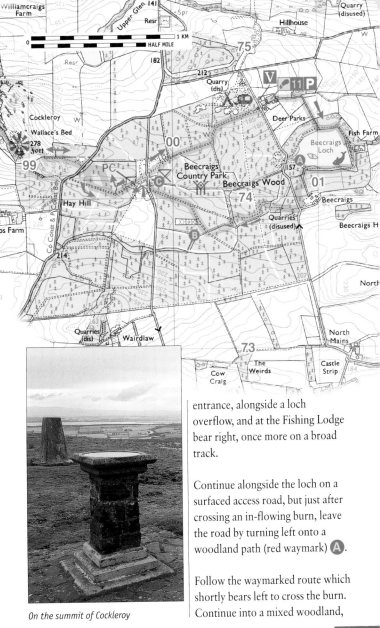

On the summit of Cockleroy

entrance, alongside a loch overflow, and at the Fishing Lodge bear right, once more on a broad track.

Continue alongside the loch on a surfaced access road, but just after crossing an in-flowing burn, leave the road by turning left onto a woodland path (red waymark) Ⓐ.

Follow the waymarked route which shortly bears left to cross the burn. Continue into a mixed woodland,

Mill pond, Bal Vormie, Beercraigs Country Park

soon walking parallel with a surfaced lane. At a signpost, cross the lane and continue further into woodland (signposted for Bal Vormie).

The track soon crosses another footbridge and rises gently to meet another track. Here continue following red waymarks through a delightful area of woodland where the stillness is disturbed only by the sound of birds and running water.

At the next large signpost, just before a broad forest trail, bear left (red and blue waymarks) and follow a track through the plantation. The trail comes out to meet a rough vehicle track, near a large cleared area. Turn right and soon pass an area set aside for archery **B**.

Continue to meet another track (once more signposted for Bal Vormie). Bear left, now following a broad forest trail alongside which there are good examples of fungal growth.

The forest trail leads to a wooden gate giving onto a road. Turn right just before the gate and walk through to a car park at Bal Vormie **C**. Cross the road at the car park entrance and go forward past Mill Pond, now following a route waymarked with pale blue arrows.

The route now turns out to ascend Cockleroy, an extension that can be omitted, as it returns to Bal Vormie. Children (and parents) may well find the nearby adventure play area a preferred option.

Distant views from the top of **Cockleroy** include North Berwick Law, 36 miles (58km) distant, Lammermuir Hills, 40 miles (64km), Ben Cleuch in the Ochil Hills, 17 miles (27km) and Goat Fell (Arran), 66 miles (106km).

Pass toilets and keep forward, once more heading into woodland. When a waymark sends the route abruptly to the right, leave the main trail and follow a narrow woodland path, crossing a marshy section on boardwalks, and finally emerging at another road.

Cross to another path opposite, and walk up the forest edge to a stile on the right giving permissive access to the grassy hill of Cockleroy. A fine view unfolds

Bird's-foot-trefoil

during the ascent of the Forth bridges and Linlithgow Loch, palace and church.

Go back down to the forest, and turn left to retrace the route to the road. Cross to the gate opposite and shortly, within the woodland, when the path forks, branch right, following a woodland path, partly on boardwalks, to meet a forest trail near a waymark. Turn left and return to Bal Vormie car park.

Cross the car park and in its far corner join a broad track (signposted for the Park Centre). This leads up past the adventure play area (and a seasonal snack bar, closed Mondays and Tuesdays).

Continue along a broad, stony forest trail that leads out to a surfaced lane at the edge of a caravan site. Go forward to a road. Cross with care into the lane opposite and soon return to the visitor centre car park.

> **?** *Can you discover what the record is for an individual rainbow trout caught in Beecraigs Loch?*

12 *Aberlady Bay Nature Reserve*

START Aberlady
DISTANCE 3¾ miles (6km)
TIME 2 hours
PARKING Reserve entrance
ROUTE FEATURES Duneland paths, scrub, seashore

Anyone wanting to begin the study of natural history could not find a better place to start. The Aberlady Nature Reserve is blessed with over 500 plant species, a breeding ground for terns, and is visited by a wide range of passage and sedentary birds – you could also see the occasional stoat. Take a picnic and enjoy it on the beach.

Set off across the long footbridge spanning Peffer Burn, entering the reserve on the other side.

A clear path leads through scrubland to reedy Marl Loch, a good place to sit patiently to see what appears.

Beyond the loch, the path, initially red gravel, runs alongside a fence, and leads up towards the Gullane Links Golf Course. Signposts direct the route onwards: when the gravel ends a grassy path continues the route.

The abundance of flowers is plainly evident throughout the

Aberlady Bay Nature Reserve is of major importance for those who study wild flowers. Over 540 species have been recorded here, including ten national rarities, and almost 100 that are locally scarce. The summer months bring in a wide range of birds including whimbrel, grasshopper warblers, short-eared owl, green sandpiper, peregrine and red-throated diver. Present all the time are curlew, greenfinch, reed bunting, linnet, oystercatcher, redshank, lapwing, heron, herring and black-headed gulls and shelduck.

PUBLIC TRANSPORT Buses to start
REFRESHMENTS Aberlady
PUBLIC TOILETS At start
ORDNANCE SURVEY MAPS Explorer 351 (Dunbar & North Berwick), Landranger 66 (Edinburgh & Midlothian area)

Gullane Bay

Hummell
Rocks

Bleaching
Rocks

Mean High Water

PC
P

Gullane Point **B**

83

Maggie's
Loup

King's
Chair

The
Old Man

Gullane
Hill 69

Jophies Neuk

46

Dunes

Gullane Links

Gullane
Sands

82

C

Yellow Mires

A

Brand's
W·Well

A198

Aberlady
Bay

Upper Mires

Gala Law MS

47

Luffness
Links

CH

Aberlady Bay
Nature Reserve

81

Marl
Loch

Aberlady Point

Peffer Burn

FB

P 12

PC

Dovecot

Luffness
House

Earthworks

Fish Ponds
(rems of)

CH

Kilspindie

6

Friars W
(rems of)

Bickerton
Strip

eepfolds

Kilspindie
Castle
(rems of)

4

80

War
Meml

PO

Aberlady

12

Hotel

A6137

Aberlady
Mains

0   1 KM

HALF MILE

13

Two Gates

Maggie's
Waas
Wood

Aberlady Bay Nature Reserve WALK 12 **45**

walk, with the lovely blue flowers of viper's bugloss prominent during summer months along with scentless mayweed, ragwort, bindweed, vetch, sea aster and the occasional woody nightshade, which is also known as bittersweet.

At a crosspath **A** keep forward, crossing the golf course with care and heading for rocky Gullane Point **B**.

Bear left and walk back down the edge of the bay, at the base of the sand dunes, but only as far as a

Marl Loch is an open and maintained water habitat, where the spread of vegetation is controlled. This is a good place to see mute swans, coot and mallard.

footpath sign directing the route inwards at the edge of a breeding ground for terns **C**. Arctic/common terns can be quite aggressive when breeding, so it is advisable to keep a safe distance from them – and be prepared to duck!

The sandy path eventually leads back to the crosspath. Turn right and retrace the outward route to Peffer Burn. ●

? *See how many different plant species you can spot.*

Marl loch, Aberlady Bay

Threipmuir and Harlaw Reservoirs

START	Balerno (Redford Wood)
DISTANCE	3¾ miles (6.1km)
TIME	2 hours
PARKING	Adjoining Redford Wood
ROUTE FEATURES	Reservoirs, moorland, stiles, woodland

This easy walk tours two Pentland reservoirs on level paths that are a delight to walk. Not included as part of the walk, but a worthy addition, is Red Moss Nature Reserve, a short distance down the road towards Redford Bridge: this remarkable reserve has Edinburgh's only example of a raised bog, and some rare plant species.

Leave the Threipmuir car park and turn left along a broad track that shortly bends left and follows a clear route through gates to reach the edge of Threipmuir Reservoir (ignore the turning to Easter Bavelaw Farm).

At the far side of Threipmuir Reservoir the track bends right to cross a ford below the overflow channel. Do not continue along this track but instead, keep left, walking towards a nearby bridge, and there turn left onto a long straight track (accompanying footpath in adjacent woodland of

Harlaw and Threipmuir Reservoirs were built and enlarged between 1848 and 1890. They feed into the Water of Leith, which supplied power for a number of mills along its length. The reservoirs were able to ensure a year-round supply of water to the mills. Today all the industry has gone, but the reservoirs have a new role for wildlife and recreation.

Scots pine and spruce) alongside Harlaw Reservoir **A**.

On the far side of Harlaw Reservoir turn right to pass the ranger centre and right again on a lovely wooded

---

PUBLIC TRANSPORT Buses to Balerno
REFRESHMENTS Balerno
PUBLIC TOILETS At visitor centre
ORDNANCE SURVEY MAPS Explorer 344 (Pentland Hills, Penicuik & West Lothian), Landranger 65 (Falkirk & West Lothian)

path until it rounds the thumb-like projection at the eastern edge of the reservoir **B**. Here, turn left over a ladder-stile onto a path signposted to Black Springs.

The ongoing path crosses rough pasture to a stile where it enters an elongated enclosure planted with young trees (2002). On the far

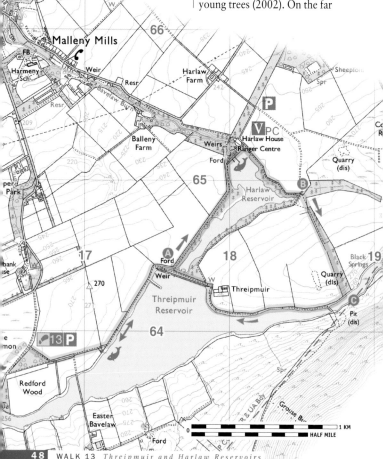

side, two step-stiles either side of a small enclosure allow the path to continue through more new plantings, finally reaching the long 'tributary' of Threipmuir Reservoir at Black Springs **C**.

Cross another stile and follow a delightful water's edge path, later in and out of a small woodland to reach the ruins of Threipmuir Farm. Here, cross the dam embankment and turn left onto a lower track that leads back to the ford and footbridge encountered earlier in the walk. Keep to the track, or, a few strides along it, turn in through a wall gap and immediately left through the end of woodland to the bridge.

Over the bridge and go left to retrace the outward route to the Threipmuir car park.

[Walkers wanting to visit the Red Moss Nature Reserve can divert to it just as the return track bends right to the

? *Can you find a blue squirrel?*

car park. Here a signposted path (for Nine Mile Burn) cuts through the edge of Redford Wood and emerges directly opposite the entrance to the nature reserve. A short boarded walk leads round the nature reserve, which boasts a fantastic range of plant and birdlife including the insectivorous sundew and the rather squishy sphagnum moss bog.]

Threipmuir Reservior

14 *Allermuir Hill and Caerketton Hill*

START Boghall Farm
DISTANCE 3¾ miles (6.2km)
TIME 2–2½ hours
PARKING Car park at start
ROUTE FEATURES Hillside tracks, hill summits, very steep descents

This delightful circuit not only allows a good introduction to walking in the Pentland Hills but provides a stunning view of Edinburgh and the Firth of Forth (and beyond). The walking is of the highest order and the views throughout are excellent and well worth the effort.

🖊 Begin from the car park at Boghall Farm by walking through a gate in a corner and then heading along an enclosed path that wends a way around the farm. It finally emerges at a broad track. Turn right and walk up as far as a cottage Ⓐ.

The track forks at the cottage. Keep left, passing sheep pens and go through a metal gate and onto a vehicle track heading up Boghall Glen.

The track climbs steadily into the glen, but later levels off for a while, running forward to a gate and stile. For a time, beyond the gate, the track continues more or less horizontally, but then starts ascending again to another gate/stile, with the rounded summit of Allermuir Hill directly ahead.

The ongoing track becomes intermittent and then peters out altogether, but the objective is a pair of ladder-stiles. Cross both stiles, and a short way on when the ongoing path forks, keep left.

Gradually the path works a way round to another stile below

PUBLIC TRANSPORT Buses to start
REFRESHMENTS Pub at Goldburn and Flotterstone Bridge
PUBLIC TOILETS None on route
ORDNANCE SURVEY MAPS Explorer 344 (Pentland Hills, Penicuik & West Linton), Landranger 66 (Edinburgh & Midlothian area)

Windy Door Nick **B**, a neat bealach between Allermuir Hill and Caerketton Hill.

Walk up to the bealach and over a stile where the spread of Edinburgh suddenly bursts into view. This is a view that will accompany much of the rest of the walk.

In the upper part of **Boghall Glen** the terrain noticeably changes to rough grazing where the hardy black-faced sheep roam the hillsides, and where grouse also breed in the heather.

Turn left on a clear path that rises beside a fenceline to the top of Allermuir Hill, the summit of which is marked by a trig pillar and a topograph identifying much of the surrounding (and distant) landmarks. [*The ascent of Allermuir Hill can be omitted.*]

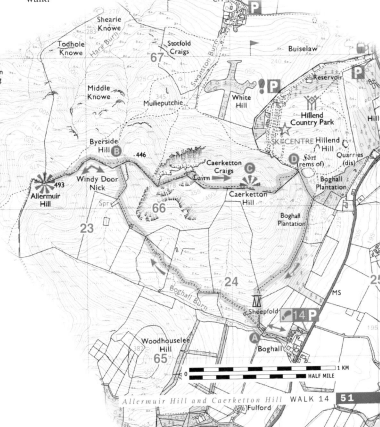

View over Edinburgh from Allermuir Hill

Return to Windy Door Nick, and then start up a path opposite that leads past a fenced area of low-lying juniper bushes before rising to the high point, marked by a large pile of stones, above Caerketton Craigs.

Continue across the summit, always following a fenceline to reach Caerketton Hill **C**. Cross this summit, too, the path flanked by heather and bilberry and the views of Edinburgh and out along the Firth of Forth to North Berwick Law and Bass Rock, constant companions.

From Caerketton Hill the path descends very steeply. When it swings left to head towards the top of the Midlothian Artificial Ski Slope, leave it, continuing to descend steeply beside a fence. [*Anyone not happy on this steep descent can go left along the path towards the ski slope, and then bear right to head back to the foot of the steep descent.*]

The view from these summits was one much admired by **Robert Louis Stevenson**, author of the book *Kidnapped*, a son of Edinburgh, but one who spent his last years far away on the Pacific island of Samoa – longing for his 'Hills of Home', as he described the Pentlands.

At the bottom of the descent , cross a stile in a fence corner and turn right onto a path (signposted to Boghall) at the edge of Hillend Country Park.

Follow a grassy path, and when it forks, keep alongside the adjacent fence, descending steeply once more through banks or gorse and bracken. At the foot of the descent, cross another stile, continuing in the direction of Boghall, and now follow an intermittently boggy path, seasonally overgrown and with protruding tree roots to trip the unwary. When not concentrating on the placement of one's feet, this is a good place to keep an eye open for orchids.

The path leads to a stile spanning a fence. Over this keep descending the hillside, obliquely, staying roughly parallel with a fence on the left, to go down to reach a kissing-gate. Ignore the gate and continue down beside the fence, closely pressed beside it by gorse.

> The upper sections of Boghall Glen are a favoured haunt of red grouse. See if you can spot any.

At the bottom, turn left through another kissing-gate (signposted to the car park). Descend a field edge and turn through another gate to walk in front of a cottage . Bear left on joining a broad track. Follow this to the edge of Boghall Farm, and there turn left returning to the car park along the enclosed path used at the start of the walk. ●

Juniper bushes and Allermuir Hill

15 *Dalkeith Country Park*

START Dalkeith	
DISTANCE 4 miles (6.4km)	
TIME 2 hours	
PARKING Dalkeith and in country park (free)	
ROUTE FEATURES Woodland trails, estate roads, farm fields	

An ancient woodland forms the basis of this enjoyable country park. Children will love the massive adventure playground, but there is much throughout the estate for everyone to enjoy. There is a charge for admission to the park during summer months.

In Dalkeith Country Park

Inside the park gates bear left, but before reaching Dalkeith House, go left down steep steps, noting near the top an ice house, which would have served the original mansion.

At the bottom of the steps, ignore a footbridge ahead, and bear right on a gently rising path that leads around the rear of Dalkeith House and then descends again. The path levels as it runs towards Montagu Bridge.

PUBLIC TRANSPORT Buses to Dalkeith
REFRESHMENTS Dalkeith and in country park
PUBLIC TOILETS In country park
PLAY AREA Adventure play area in park
ORDNANCE SURVEY MAPS Explorer 350 (Edinburgh, Musselburgh & Queensferry), Landranger 66 (Edinburgh & Midlothian area)

Near the foot of the bridge, bear right on a wide path, heading away from the river, and rising eventually to emerge close to the front of Dalkeith House.

At the top of the climb turn left onto a surfaced lane, but shortly branch left to follow a track that leads over Montagu Bridge, with a fine view either side of the River North Esk.

Dalkeith House was built in the Palladian style under the instructions of Anne, 1st Duchess of Buccleuch around 1701, and is unmatched in Scotland. The house has seen numerous uses since the family moved out in 1918: it has been an army barracks, estate office, headquarters for a computer organisation and is now the Scottish campus for the University of Wisconsin in North America.

Beyond the bridge stay on the main driveway and take the first major turning on the right **A** with the open area of Deanhead Park now on the left.

The track continues between Deanhead Park and Howlands Park, its sides decked with a wide range of flowers and shrubs including cotton thistle, ragwort,

 Although part of the **woodlands at Dalkeith** have been managed commercially in recent times, there are still substantial remains of ancient oak woodland that has been standing here for centuries and would have been walked by the likes of King Charles I and Oliver Cromwell. The last major extraction of timber was used to build a ship, the Great Michael, in 1528.

broad-leaved willow herb, selfheal, hardheads, elder, red campion, bush and tufted vetch. Continue following the main track, ignoring diversions, as it eases on through woodlands of beech and sycamore.

After a short rise, the ongoing track forks. **B** Here, at a blue-topped waymark, bear right, following a woodland path for about 400 yds (364m) to a point where another blue waymark sends the route

? *Can you find a 'marble' basin on this walk*

Dalkeith House

Montagu Bridge, Dalkeith Country Park

right. Here, leave the waymarked route and go forward along a field-edge path, and passing beneath overhead powerlines.

Keep following the field-edge path, which later broadens and runs on to a track junction. Turn right and cross Smeaton Bridge **C**.

Over the bridge bear left on a surfaced road and walk up to a T-junction. Turn right, and when the lane forks, bear right again along an unenclosed road. The land use differs here, and so too does the range of wild flowers. Now the white daisy-like flower of scentless mayweed appears along with the perfumed pineapple weed, and poppies. Further along the road a new planted hedgerow is developing and contains an interesting and colourful mix of shrubs including berberis, hawthorn, beech and dog-rose.

The road eventually leads to a bridge giving back into the country park **D**. On re-entering the park, note the circular conservatory on the left, and then go forward through the old stables courtyard where there is now a shop and cafeteria. On the other side continue to follow the main driveway, which leads past the adventure playground and out of the park at the edge of Dalkeith town centre.

16 Monks Rig and West Kip

START	Nine Mile Burn
DISTANCE	4¼ miles (7km)
TIME	2 hours
PARKING	Nine Mile Burn
ROUTE FEATURES	Moorland paths, long ascents, steep ascent and descent (optional)

West Kip is more of an addition than an inclusive part of this walk, but its ascent, in spite of what appears to be a formidable climb, is straightforward, and its summit an excellent viewpoint. The approach rises steadily to Cap Law, returning by a delightful circuitous route by Braid Law. Save this for a clear day.

The Font Stone, Monks Rig

👣 Leave the parking area at Nine Mile Burn by walking through a nearby gate along a signposted path for Balerno by Monks Rig and Braid Law. Go forward along the bottom edge of a hill pasture, and on the far side, turn left now climbing beside a wall.

At the top of the pasture, cross a stile and turn right to another gate, and there go left, climbing once more (signposted for Monks Rig), now beside a fencline.

Keep on as far as a step-stile on the right **A**, and over this go across to

PUBLIC TRANSPORT Buses Nine Mile Burn road junction
REFRESHMENTS Pubs at Carlops and Flotterstone Bridge
PUBLIC TOILETS None on route
ORDNANCE SURVEY MAPS Explorer 344 (Pentland Hills, Penicuik & West Lothian), Landranger 66 (Edinburgh & Midlothian area)

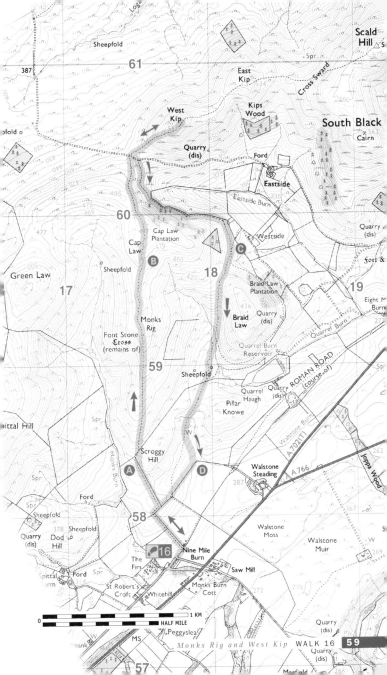

Monks Rig and West Kip WALK 16

Windblown trees, Braid Hill

a wall, beyond which the long steady ascent of Monks Rig awaits.

The path up the hill continues easily, dotted with the bright yellow eyes of tormentil, one of the few wild flowers that can survive in this windswept landscape.

With no deviation, the grassy route continues towards the dome of

Half-way up Monks Rig is the **Font Stone**, presumably so-called because it has become something of a receptacle for small goodwill offerings, but is in reality a cross-base that would have been a wayside marker for the itinerant monks who would have pioneered this route between valleys.

Cap Law, with the shapely cone of West Kip peering over its shoulder.

Approaching Cap Law, the path divides **B**; bear right on a gently descending path that curves round to intercept a clear farm access track below West Kip. Head for this and decide whether the ascent of West Kip is to be tackled. [*Omitting West Kip takes 880 yds (800m) from the walk along with 310 ft (95m) of ascent and descent.*]

The way up West Kip is well trodden and its summit a fine vantage point, making the ascent well worth the effort. The descent follows the line of ascent.

Back at the broad access track, cross to a stile giving onto a grassy path (signposted for Nine Mile Burn by Braid Law) that curves, descending gently, around the gathering grounds of Eastside Burn, crossing a couple of stiles on the way.

Eventually the accompanying fenceline ends. Keep going, and when the track forks near a right-of-way signpost **C** bear right to go through a bealach (a low gap) to the north-west of Braid Law.

Cross the bealach, and soon start descending through bracken to cross a burn. The path runs on to cross a stile and wall, beyond which a grassy path, parallel with a

Kestrels may often be seen hovering above the moorland. Can you spot any?

fence on the left, leads across to another stile. Over this turn left downfield, bearing a little to the right lower down to reach a right-of-way signpost **D**.

From the signpost, bear right alongside a fence on the left, to join the outward route at a stile and gate at the foot of Monks Rig. Go forward beside a wall for 100 yds (91m). Cross another stile, and go down a field and at the bottom turn right to return to the starting point of the walk at Nine Mile Burn. ●

The Kips, Pentland Hills

17 Carlops and North Esk Reservoir

START Carlops
DISTANCE 4½ miles (7.2km)
HEIGHT GAIN 755 ft (230m)
TIME 2 hours
PARKING Car park at Carlops
ROUTE FEATURES Farm tracks and moorland paths, steep climb

Put simply, this is a delightful walk into the bosomy folds of the Pentland Hills; peaceful wandering is the principal motive, and this agreeable circuit, which in spite of a little demanding ascent, is a fine excuse for a day in the hills – if you need one.

🥾 Leave the car park opposite the parish church and walk up the minor road opposite (signposted 'Buteland by the Borestane'). When the surfaced lane swings left to Carlopshill Farm, keep forward (waymarked) on a broad stony track heading into the lush folds of the Pentlands, a sudden and acceptable transformation.

Carlops Parish church

The track goes through a metal gate and round to pass Fairliehope Farm, beyond which it ascends gently to pass a small plantation of mixed woodland, where the ascent finally ends. Now North Esk Reservoir is in view.

The track then winds round to reach the waterman's cottage at the reservoir **A**. Just before the

PUBLIC TRANSPORT Buses to Carlops
REFRESHMENTS Pub in Carlops
PUBLIC TOILETS None on route
ORDNANCE SURVEY MAPS Explorer 344 (Pentland Hills, Penicuik & West Lothian), Landranger 65 (Falkirk & West Lothian)

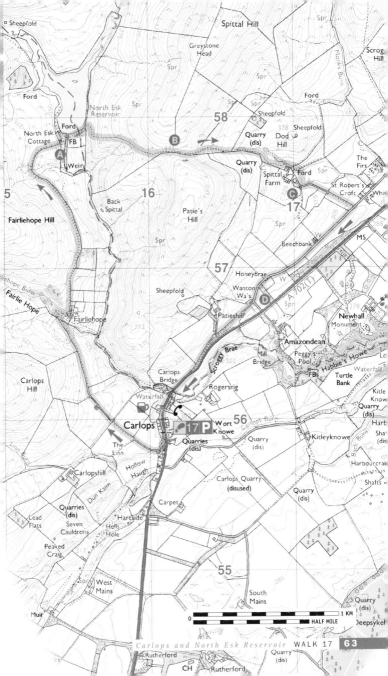

Sheepfold

Spittal Hill

Greystone
Head

Scrog
Hill

Monk's Burn

Spr

Ford

Ford

North Esk Reservoir

58

Sheepfold

Ford

Sheepfold

Quarry
(dis)

Dod
Hill

378

Sheepfold

North Esk
Cottage

A

FB

Ford

B

Weir

The
Firs

Quarry
(dis)

St Robert's
Croft

Whi

Spittal
Farm

C

17

5

Fairliehope Hill

16

Back
Spittal

Patie's
Hill

Beechbank

MS

57

Honeybrae

A 702(T)

Wanton
Wa's

D

388

Fairlie Hope

Fairliehope

392

Sheepfold

Patieshill

Mill
Bridge

Newhall
Monument

278

Carlops
Bridge

Scroggy Brae

302

Rogersrig

Amazondean

Peggy's
Pool

Habbie's Howe

Waterfall

FBs

Turtle
Bank

Kitle
Know

Carlops
Hill

Waterfall

Carlops

17 P

W ort
Knowe

56

Carlops Burn

Quarry
(dis)

Kitleyknowe

Quarry
(dis)

Hart

Sha

The
Linn

Quarries
(dis)

Hollow
Haugh

Quarries
(dis)

Quarry
(dis)

Carlops Quarry
(disused)

Quarry
(dis)

Harbourcrai

Shafts

Carlopshill

Dun Kaim

Hartside

Hell's
Hole

Carpet

Lead
Flats

Seven
Cauldrons

Peaked
Craig

West
Mains

55

South
Mains

Quarry
(dis)

Muir

0   HALF MILE   1 KM

Deepsyke

Rutherford

CH

Rutherford

Quarry
(dis)

The **North Esk Reservoir**, which has a surface area of 15.7 acres and holds 45,000,000 gallons of water, was completed in 1850. It acted as a storage tank for the mills that operated on the River North Esk in the 19th and early 20th centuries, and maintained a constant flow in the river even during summer droughts, allowing manufacturing to continue throughout the year. The chief beneficiaries of this steady supply were the paper mills at Bank Mill (which produced, as its name suggests, the paper for bank notes), Valleyfield Mill and Esk Mill.

Can you find the Wheel of Fortune?

climb left to a signpost (Nine Mile Burn), and there turn right, climbing steeply. When the path forks, take the higher of the two.

At a small rock the path levels for a while and goes forward through bracken beyond which it starts to climb again. When it forks, branch left (waymark set in rock).

The path climbs to a bealach between hills **B**, providing here the last opportunity to gaze back on the valley of the North Esk.

buildings take to a signposted route around them, which finally uses a step-stile to gain access to the dam.

Walk across the dam and on the other side cross another stile and

Continue forward to meet and follow a fence to a gate. Beyond the gate a broad hill track leads down beside a wall with the long low range of the Moorfoot and Lammermuir Hills in view in the far distance.

Go down through another gate and continue with the descending

Heading for Carlops

North Esk Reservoir in the folds of the Pentlands

track towards Spittal Farm .
The route passes to the left of the
farm, locates a wooden kissing-gate
and drops down a stony track to
meet the farm access. Turn left.

Follow the track out from Spittal
Farm to meet the quiet backroad
linking Nine Mile Burn with
Carlops. Turn right onto this, and
follow it for about half-a-mile
(800m).

Just before the road turns left to go
down to meet the A702, leave it by
turning right at Wanton Wa's **D**
onto a minor road.

When the road surfacing ends and
the ongoing track swings to the
right, leave it on the apex by going
forward onto a footpath
signposted for Carlops.

The path is seasonally overgrown
with unclear edges, and fights its
way through bracken though
speedwell, ragwort, willowherb,
dog-rose and foxgloves put in a
colourful appearance.

A few steps finally bring the path
down to meet the road, which is
followed over Carlops Bridge back
to the start.

18 *Braid Hills*

START Blackford

DISTANCE 5 miles (8km)

TIME 2–2½ hours

PARKING Car park at Blackford Pond

ROUTE FEATURES Woodland trails, burnside paths, golf course, hilltop, valley park, roads

Little more than 2 miles (3km) from the centre of Edinburgh, the area of the Braid Hills is a gem, a delightful place to walk, full of interest and with stunning views.

Begin from the small car park near Blackford Pond by turning right onto a broad track that soon passes the pond with its resident population of mallard, swans, coot and dabchick.

The path passes allotment gardens and continues around Blackford Hill, along the edge of woodland, a habitat favoured by red campion, foxglove, elder, gorse and the invasive Indian balsam. Soon, the path merges with another below Blackford Hill. Keep right, soon descending through stands of sycamore, beech, elder and hawthorn.

When the path forks, branch right, continuing to descend, now more steeply to reach a metal kissing-gate. Through this, keep left to join a level track bearing left **A**, alongside Braid Burn and passing old quarries on the left.

Carry on to reach Howe Dean Path on the right, at a Nature Reserve information panel. Here, turn right, crossing a footbridge and going up Howe Dean Path, which

PUBLIC TRANSPORT Buses to start

REFRESHMENTS In Visitor Centre (limited opening), otherwise Blackford

PLAY AREA Adjoining Blackford Pond

PUBLIC TOILETS None on route

ORDNANCE SURVEY MAPS Explorer 350 (Edinburgh, Musselburgh & Queensferry), Landranger 66 (Edinburgh and Midlothian area)

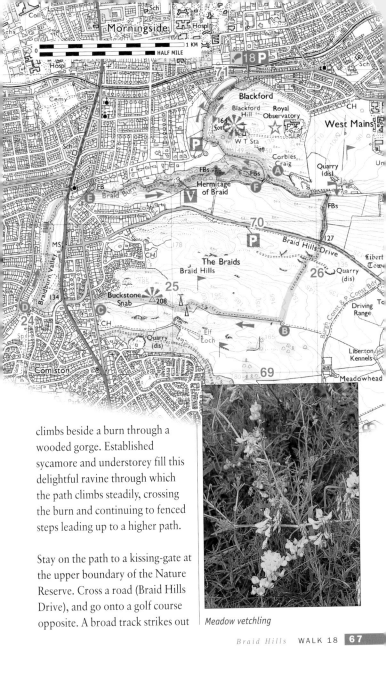

climbs beside a burn through a wooded gorge. Established sycamore and understorey fill this delightful ravine through which the path climbs steadily, crossing the burn and continuing to fenced steps leading up to a higher path.

Stay on the path to a kissing-gate at the upper boundary of the Nature Reserve. Cross a road (Braid Hills Drive), and go onto a golf course opposite. A broad track strikes out

Meadow vetchling

onto the golf course, where it is important to take care against low-flying golf balls as the route crosses a number of fairways.

When the track forks, bear left, the track now climbing a little. As the rising track turns left and abruptly ends, go forward, maintaining the original direction along a path flanked by gorse bushes. At the top of the path, keep heading the same way, now along a broad green sward, crossing more fairways finally to reach a red shale path **B**.

The view from the top of **Braid Hills** embraces notably the **Seven Hills of Edinburgh** – Arthur's Seat, Blackford Hill, Braid Hills, Calton Hill, Castle Rock, Corstorphine Hill and Craiglockhart Hill. But the extent of the panorama is unbelievable and reaches to Ben Lomond 58 miles (94km) away, Ben Vorlich 65 miles (105km), Ben More and Stob Binnein, 61 miles (98km) and 60 miles (97km) respectively.

Turn right along the shale path, soon walking alongside a wall. Here is a good place to keep an eye open for bullfinches, the male of the species boasting a deep red chest, black cap on his head and a conspicuous white rump.

Follow the red shale path, leaving it only momentarily to climb to the top of a low hill topped by a trig pillar and topograph.

Continue across the top of the hill to rejoin the red shale path, which soon starts to descend. When the path forks branch left, walk down to meet a road **C**. [*Take care emerging onto the road: there is no roadside footpath and the exit is close to a blind summit.*]

Cross the road and turn right. Take the first turning on the left (Riselaw

Blackford Pond

Crescent), and follow this round to meet an A-road (Pentland Terrace/Comiston Road). Cross and turn right, walking beside a fence for about 100 yds (91m), and then turn left into Braidburn Valley Park, bearing left to walk through an avenue of trees.

When the path merges with another, bear right and descend to meet Braid Burn once more **D**. Keep right, above the burn, crossing it at the second footbridge and turning right along a surfaced pathway. Keep an eye open here for clusters of monkey flower and forget-me-not alongside the burn and the long strandlike stems and delicate white flowers of river-water crowfoot which actually flourish in the water.

Shortly after the burn enters a culvert, walk up to park gates and turn right to a major road junction. Go into the road opposite, passing Greenbank Parish Church. Continue for about 175 yds (160m) to another junction at a roundabout, and here turn right into Braid Road.

> **The Hermitage of Braid** and its grounds were gifted to the City of Edinburgh by John McDougal, and officially opened by the then Lord Provost in June 1938. The area is thought to have been named after a former Sheriff of Edinburgh, Henri de Brad, who was a major landowner here during the 12th century.

A few strides further on, go left into the Hermitage of Braid Nature Reserve **E**. Cross a bridge spanning Braid Burn, and keep forward on a surfaced driveway that leads to the Hermitage, now housing the Visitor Centre (open afternoons only, April-September).

Continue past the visitor centre, always following the burnside path which changes banks a few times before finally passing beneath a wooden footbridge **F**.

Just after the footbridge, leave the track and bear left, up steps to a metal kissing-gate where the outward route is joined. Beyond the gate climb steadily on a stony track that soon levels as it passes through woodland.

When the track forks, bear left, descending gently, and going back past Blackford Pond to return to the start.

> *Can you find a plaque that tells about a geological discovery?*

19 *Pentland Ridge*

START Flotterstone

DISTANCE 6¾ miles (11km)

HEIGHT GAIN 1542 ft (470m)

TIME 4 hours

PARKING Flotterstone

ROUTE FEATURES Hill farms, upland tracks, lanes, reservoirs, steep climbs and descents

The modest elevation of the Pentlands, lying so close to the heart of a great city, is deceptive. The main ridge featured in this walk is exposed to the elements. It doesn't extend to the highest summit in the Pentlands, though strong walkers could easily include it. This is not a walk to attempt in poor visibility.

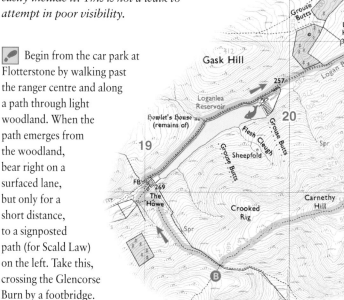

Begin from the car park at Flotterstone by walking past the ranger centre and along a path through light woodland. When the path emerges from the woodland, bear right on a surfaced lane, but only for a short distance, to a signposted path (for Scald Law) on the left. Take this, crossing the Glencorse Burn by a footbridge.

PUBLIC TRANSPORT Buses to Flotterstone Bridge

REFRESHMENTS Pub at Flotterstone

PICNIC AREA Near start (small)

PUBLIC TOILETS At start

ORDNANCE SURVEY MAPS Explorer 344 (Pentland Hills, Penicuik & West Linton), Landranger 66 (Edinburgh & Midlothian area)

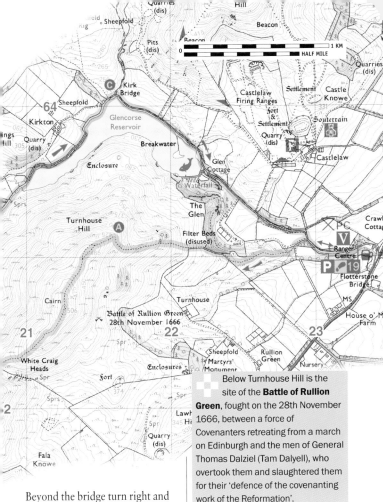

Below Turnhouse Hill is the site of the **Battle of Rullion Green**, fought on the 28th November 1666, between a force of Covenanters retreating from a march on Edinburgh and the men of General Thomas Dalziel (Tam Dalyell), who overtook them and slaughtered them for their 'defence of the covenanting work of the Reformation'.

Beyond the bridge turn right and climb to gain the end of an obvious ridge that leads to the first summit on the main ridge, Turnhouse Hill Ⓐ.

After Turnhouse Hill the ridge flows on, undulating, each peak distinct from the rest. A steady descent to a neat col, crossing an intermediate fence, preludes a climb onto Carnethy Hill, surmounted by a Bronze Age cairn.

Continue to follow the ridge as once more it descends to another

Carnethy Hill, in spite of its modest elevation, provides a superb vantage point, with extensive views over the region of Fife, the nearby Moorfoot Hills, and as far as Bass Rock in the Firth of Forth.

bealach (pass) **B**, this time one much-used as a link between Balerno and Penicuik. This is the Kirk Road, and it descends directly to the head of Loganlea Reservoir.

Now all that remains is easy walking, through beautiful

landscapes along the length of Loganlea Reservoir and along Logan Burn to meet Glencorse Reservoir.

At Kirk Bridge **C**, the road bends right and takes the walk back to the start at Flotterstone. ●

The hillsides of the Pentlands make a superb hunting ground for buzzards. See if you can spot any.

Along the Pentland Ridge (Carnethy Hill)

Scald Hill

20

START Balerno (Redford Wood)
DISTANCE 7 miles (11.5km)
TIME 4–4½ hours
PARKING Adjoining Redford Wood
ROUTE FEATURES Moorland, hills, steep ascents and descent

This splendid climb to the highest point of the Pentland Hills needs a clear day and plenty of refreshments. The ascent is gradual, until the foot of West Kip is reached, and then it becomes a delightful switchback before crossing Scald Hill. Once the descent to the edge of Loganlea Reservoir is over, there follows a splendid continuation through the steep-sided valley of Green Cleugh.

Leave the Threipmuir Reservoir car park and walk right and immediately left on the road leading down to the Red Moss Nature Reserve and the Bavelaw Reserve, both of which are worth exploring on less demanding days.

Cross Redford Bridge, and continue up the tree-lined track beyond to a junction **A**. Turn right (signposted for Nine Mile Burn and Carlops). Pass through a gate and turn left along another access track to a stile. Over the stile, climb beside a wall to another stile.

Now simply follow the ongoing track uphill, parallel with a wall, and then breaking out onto the smooth-flanked Pentlands, passing around Hare Hill, crossing Logan Burn and then climbing to the foot

The Pentland Hills, now embraced within a regional park, were the 'Hills of Home' of **Robert Louis Stevenson**, who summed them up magnificently, and, alas, accurately, when he wrote: 'Blows the wind to-day, and the sun and the rain are flying.' They are a superb place for those seeking solitude and tranquillity, or merely the pleasure of being among the hills.

PUBLIC TRANSPORT Buses to Balerno
REFRESHMENTS Balerno
PUBLIC TOILETS At visitor centre
ORDNANCE SURVEY MAPS Explorer 344 (Pentland Hills, Penicuik & West Lothian), Landranger 65 (Falkirk & West Lothian)

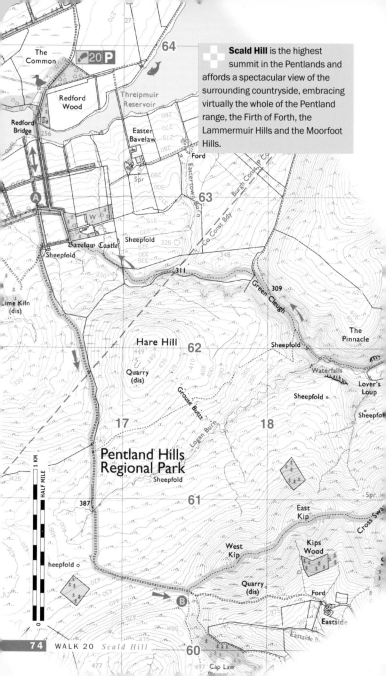

Scald Hill is the highest summit in the Pentlands and affords a spectacular view of the surrounding countryside, embracing virtually the whole of the Pentland range, the Firth of Forth, the Lammermuir Hills and the Moorfoot Hills.

The Common

P 20 P

Redford Wood

Threipmuir Reservoir

Redford Bridge

256

Easter Bavelaw

Ford

Spr

64

63

Eastertown Burn

Co Const Bdy

Burgh Const

Bavelaw Castle

Sheepfold

Sheepfold

311

Green Cleugh

309

Lime Kiln (dis)

Hare Hill

449

62

Sheepfold

The Pinnacle

Quarry (dis)

Waterfalls

Lover's Loup

Grouse Butts

Sheepfold

Sheepfold

17

Logan Burn

18

Pentland Hills Regional Park

Sheepfold

387

61

East Kip

Cross Swa

Kips Wood

West Kip

heepfold

Quarry (dis)

Ford

Eastside

B

Eastside b.

60

Cap Law

1 KM

HALF MILE

0

of a clear path rising very steeply onto West Kip **B**.

The ascent of West Kip is not so demanding as it appears end-on, and the summit is soon reached.

Beyond, a clear path descends towards East Kip, crosses this lower summit and then descends more steeply to the bealach below Scald Hill. Here the path forks; branch left and climb steeply onto Scald Hill.

From the trig pillar on the summit of Scald Hill head steeply down to meet the Kirk Road at the bealach between Scald Hill and Carnethy Hill **C**. Cross a stile and turn left heading downhill to the head of Loganlea Reservoir.

At the bottom of the descent go left at a fence corner and along a path beside a burn **D**.

Continue through Green Cleugh,

Threipmuir Reservoir from Redford Bridge

climbing easily to a stile, and over this press on tightly sandwiched between Hare Hill on the left and Black Hill on the right.

Gradually the steep sides relax, and the path swings left around the base of Hare Hill, heading for a wooded area around the site of Bavelaw Castle.

A stile gives access to a beech driveway, which shortly bends left and then right, and rejoins the outward route at the head of the long beech driveway used on the outward route. Follow this down to Redford Bridge and walk out along the access road to the start. ●

> **?** One of the popular birds to patrol the Pentlands during the summer months is the wheatear. See if you can spot any.

Further Information

Walking Safety

Always take with you both warm and waterproof clothing and sufficient food and drink. Wear suitable footwear, i.e. strong walking boots or shoes that give a good grip over stony ground, on slippery slopes and in muddy conditions. Try to obtain a local weather forecast and bear it in mind before you start. Do not be afraid to abandon your proposed route and return to your starting point in the event of a sudden and unexpected deteriorationin the weather.

All the walks described in this book will be safe to do, given due care and respect, even during the winter. Indeed, a crisp, fine winter day often provides perfect walking conditions, with firm ground underfoot and a clarity of light unique to that time of the year.

The most difficult hazard likely to be encountered is mud, especially when walking along woodland and field paths, farm tracks and bridleways – the latter in particular can often get churned up by cyclists and horses. In summer, an additional difficulty may be narrow and overgrown paths, particularly along the edges of cultivated fields. Neither should constitute a major problem provided that the appropriate footwear is worn.

Follow the Country Code

- Enjoy the countryside and respect its life and work
- Guard against all risk of fire
- Take your litter home
- Fasten all gates
- Help to keep all water clean
- Keep your dogs under control
- Protect wildlife, plants and trees
- Keep to public paths across farmland
- Take special care on country roads
- Leave livestock, crops and machinery alone
- Make no unnecessary noise
- Use gates and stiles to cross fences, hedges and walls

(The Countryside Agency)

Useful Organisations

Forest Enterprise
31 Corstorphine Road, Edinburgh EH12 7AT. Tel: 0131 3340303; Fax: 0131 3343047.

Historic Scotland
Longmore House, Salisbury Place, Edinburgh EH9 1SH. Tel: 0131

Reaching the top of West Kip: line of ascent in background

6688800; website: www.historic-scotland.gov.uk.

National Trust for Scotland
Wemyss House, 28 Charlotte Square, Edinburgh EH2 4ET. Tel: 0131 2439300; Fax: 0131 243 9301; Email: information@nts.org.uk; Website: www.nts.org.uk.

Ordnance Survey
Romsey Road, Maybush, Southampton SO16 4GU. Tel: 02380 792912; Fax: (Public) 02380 792615; Email: custinfo@ordsvy.gov.uk; Website: www.ordsvy.gov.uk.

Pentland Hills Ranger Service
Boghall Farm, Biggar EH10 7DX. Tel: 0131 4453383.

Ramblers' Association
2nd Floor, Camelford House, 87–90 Albert Embankment, London SE1 7TW. Tel: 020 73398585; Fax: 020 7339 8501; Website: www.ramblers.org.uk.

Royal Society for the Protection of Birds (RSPB)
The Lodge, Sandy, Beds SG19 2DL. Tel: 01767 680551; Fax: 01767 692365; Website: www.rspb.org.uk

Scottish Natural Heritage
Battleby, Redgorton, Perth PH1
3EW. Tel: 01738 627921; Fax:
01738 630583; Contact: Media
enquiries, Edinburgh (Tel 0131
447 4784).

Scottish Wild Land Group
8 Hartington Place, Bruntsfield,
Edinburgh EH10 4LE. Tel: 0131
2292094.

Scottish Youth Hostels Association
7 Glebe Crescent, Stirling FK8
2JA. Tel: 01786 891400; Fax:
01786 891333; Email:
syha@syha.org.uk; Website:
www.syha.org.uk.

Local tourist information centres:
Bo'ness: 01506 826626
Edinburgh: 0131 4733800
Edinburgh Airport: 0131 3332167
Musselburgh: See Old Craighall
North Berwick: 01620 892197
Old Craighall: 0131 6536172
Penicuik: 01968 613846

Tourist organisations
Visit Scotland
23 Ravelston Terrace
Edinburgh EH4 3TP
Tel: 0131 3322433
Fax: 0131 3152906
Email: info@visitscotland.com
Website: www.visitscotland.net

Mason's mark, Linlithgow Church